OUR GOVERNMENT

National Elections

and the Political Process

Bryon Giddens-White

Heinemann
LIBRARY

Chicago, Illinois

Designed by David Poole and Calcium
Illustrations by Geoff Ward
Originated by P.T. Repro Multi Warna
Printed in China by WKT Company Limited

07 06 05
10 9 8 7 6 5 4 3 2 1

Library of Congress Cataloging-in-Publication Data
Giddens-White, Bryon.
  National elections and the political process / Bryon Giddens-White.
      p. cm. -- (Our government)
  Includes bibliographical references and index.
  ISBN 1-4034-6604-1 (hc) -- ISBN 1-4034-6609-2 (pb)
  1. Elections--United States--Juvenile literature. 2. Voting--United States--Juvenile literature. I. Title. II. Series.
  JK1978.G53 2006
  324.6'0973--dc22

                              2005008667

Acknowledgments
AP Wide World Photo pp. 15 (J. Scott Applewhite), 17 (Ron Edmonds), 18 (Ron Edmonds), 19 (Swiftvets), 23 (Ed Andrieski), 24 (Alan Diaz), 25 (Ron Edmonds), 29 (Gail Burton); Corbis pp. 4 (Bettmann), 5 (Bettmann), 6 (Bettamann), 8 (Bettmann), 16 (Dallas Morning News/Erich Schlegel), 21 (Bettmann), 27 (Reuters/Fred Prouser); Getty Images pp. 1 (Comstock Images), 14 (Hulton Archive/Kean Collection); Library of Congress p. 9; National Archive and Records Administration p. 7; North Wind Picture Archives p. 10; www.census.gov pp. 20, 26.

Cover photograph of campaign buttons reproduced with permission of Getty Images (Comstock Images.)

Every effort has been made to contact copyright holders of any material reproduced in this book. Any omissions will be rectified in subsequent printings if notice is given to the publishers.

Special thanks to Gary Barr and Paula McClain for their help in the production of this book.

Contents

Any words appearing in the text in bold, **like this**, are explained in the Glossary.

Fighting for the Right to Vote

For much of United States history, blacks have struggled to gain the same rights enjoyed by other U.S. citizens. Racism and **discrimination** often prevented blacks from participating in the democratic process. The U.S. government took few steps to fix this situation until the 1950s, when large numbers of blacks joined a mass movement to demand their **civil rights**.

A key goal of the **civil rights movement** was voting rights. For years, white officials in the South had denied many blacks the right to vote. Civil rights groups, such as the Southern Christian Leadership Conference (SCLC) and the Student Nonviolent Coordinating Committee (SNCC), tried to help blacks vote in the South.

Fannie Lou Hamer ▶ worked hard to gain voting rights for blacks. She spoke at the Democratic National Convention in 1964 and 1968.

In August of 1962, a Mississippi woman named Fannie Lou Hamer responded to a call from the SNCC (pronounced "snick"). She started to work with the group to end voting discrimination. When her employer heard about what Hamer was doing, he fired her. Hamer then worked with the SNCC full time.

Two years later, the nation was preparing for presidential elections. Before national elections take place, each state sends a group of people to **national conventions** to choose presidential candidates. Hamer became angry because she felt that the all-white group sent by Mississippi did not represent the state's black voters. She helped organize a group called the Mississippi Freedom Democratic Party (MFDP).

In front of a large television audience, Hamer spoke to convention officials and outlined the goals of the MFDP. She explained that blacks in many states were prevented from voting through illegal tests, taxes, and violent intimidation. As a result of her speech, two MFDP members were allowed to speak at the convention. Other members were seated as honorable guests.

Because of the hard work of people like Hamer and groups like SCLC and SNCC, the U.S. government took steps to eliminate racial discrimination. A year after Hamer's appearance at the national convention, President Lyndon Johnson signed the **Voting Rights Act**, which would eventually bring an end to the discrimination described by Hamer at the 1964 convention.

Nonviolence

Many people who participated in the civil rights movement, including civil rights leader Dr. Martin Luther King Jr. (left), practiced nonviolent protest. Even when they were physically attacked, nonviolent civil rights protesters refused to fight back physically. They believed nonviolence was a positive force that could change the hearts and minds of their opponents. Civil rights leaders adopted this philosophy from Mahatma Gandhi, who had used nonviolent protest to force the British to end their colonial rule of India.

Introduction to Elections

Fact File

Form of government in the United States: Representative Democracy

Election day: First Tuesday after the first Monday in November

Minimum voting age: 18 (established by the 26th Amendment)

Year all men gained the right to vote: 1870, with the 15th Amendment

Year all women gained the right to vote: 1920, with the 19th Amendment

Current major political parties: Democratic Party and Republican Party

During the spring of 1787, a group of men gathered to make a plan for the United States government. The written document that they created is called the U.S. **Constitution**. The government created by the U.S. Constitution is a republic, or **representative democracy**.

A democracy is a form of government in which the people hold power. In a representative democracy, citizens exercise their power by choosing people to represent them in the government. In a large country like the United States, it would be too difficult to have citizens vote on every issue. Instead, they choose representatives by voting in periodic elections.

As you have read, the United States has not always allowed its citizens to have equal voting rights. For a long time, only a small group of

individuals were allowed to vote. Over time, however, citizens fought for and won the right to vote. In the next section, you will read more about the expansion of **suffrage**, or the right to vote, in the United States.

◀ The U.S. Constitution grants states the power to conduct elections as they see fit, with some limitations from the federal government.

◀ In 1787, 55 **delegates**—including present and future leaders George Washington, Benjamin Franklin, and James Madison—met in Philadelphia. Their efforts produced the U.S. Constitution, a document that still directs the United States government today.

Who Can Vote

Early in the history of the United States, relatively few people could vote. As states joined the **Union**, lawmakers tended to restrict voting rights to white males who owned property.

Gradually, the right to vote was extended. After slavery was outlawed in the United States, the government passed a series of **amendments** to the Constitution. Among these was the Fifteenth Amendment, passed in 1870, which gave former male slaves the right to vote. However, many years would pass before many blacks, especially in the South, would get the chance to exercise this new right.

Election officials used different techniques to prevent blacks from voting. These included giving former slaves literacy tests to determine whether they could read and write (most former slaves could not read because teaching slaves had been against the law), and creating voting taxes that were too expensive for former slaves to pay.

As blacks pressed for voting rights during the civil rights movement, the U.S. government slowly began to remove these barriers. In 1964, the 24th Amendment made the voting tax illegal. The Voting Rights Act of 1965 also made it more difficult for states to place restrictions on who

▼ President Lyndon Johnson signs the 1965 Voting Rights bill into law.

could vote. In addition, the act gave the federal government the power to **register** citizens whom the states refused to put on their voting lists.

While all men were granted the right to vote by the Fifteenth Amendment in 1870, women waited another 50 years to vote in most states. During the mid-1800s, women fought hard for the right to vote. The women's suffrage movement gained strength in 1848, when its leaders held a convention in Seneca Falls, New York. There, convention attendees drafted The Declaration of Sentiments, modeled after The Declaration of Independence. The document called for women's equal rights in areas such as education, property, and voting.

Not everyone was convinced that women should have the same rights as men. But in 1920, with the passage of the Nineteenth Amendment, women finally won the right to vote.

Since then, the government has extended voting rights even further. In 1971, **Congress** passed the 26th Amendment, which lowered the voting age from 21 to 18.

▲ Women march in New York City on May 6, 1912, demanding the right to vote.

Levels of Government

Voters in the United States elect representatives to many levels of government in local, state, and national elections. One reason why the United States has several levels of government has to do with its history.

During the Revolutionary War (1775-83), the colonists fought to become independent of Great Britain because they believed the British government was abusing its power over them. After winning the war, the nation's **founders** worked to ensure that the new government would not do the same.

The authors of the Constitution were careful not to give too much power to the national government of the United States. They gave certain powers to the national government, but others they assigned to the state governments. This division of power is

▼ The authors of the Constitution carefully studied other governments, including that of Athens, in ancient Greece. Because Athens had a relatively small population, a form of **direct democracy** was possible, and citizens were directly involved in the decision-making process. The founders decided this process would not be practical in the United States.

called a **federal system** of government.

Under the federal system, U.S. citizens elect representatives to the national government. They also elect representatives to their own states. The national government and most state governments have the same three-part structure. Each has a **legislative branch** that makes laws, an **executive branch** that carries out and enforces the laws, and a **judicial branch** that interprets the laws.

In both national and state elections, citizens elect people to represent them in the legislative branch. They also vote for the leaders of the executive branch—a president at the national level and **governors** at the state level. In some states, citizens elect judges to the judicial branch. At the national level, the Constitution gives the president the power to nominate judges.

In addition to voting in national and state elections, citizens also have the opportunity to elect representatives to local governments. It is estimated that there are more than 84,000 local governments in the United States.

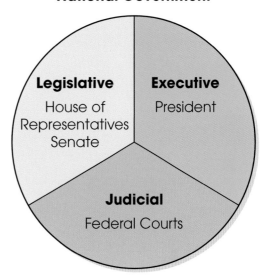

National Government

Legislative — House of Representatives, Senate
Executive — President
Judicial — Federal Courts

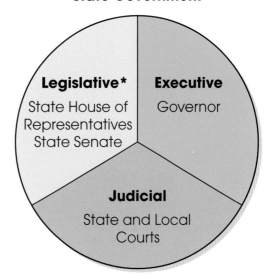

State Government

Legislative* — State House of Representatives, State Senate
Executive — Governor
Judicial — State and Local Courts

The state of Nebraska has only one house of Congress.

▲ The structure of most state governments is very similar to the national government.

11

Levels of Government

As you have read, the United States has three levels of government: national, state, and local. The following maps describe some of the features of state and local governments.

State Governments

The structure of state governments is similar to the national government. Each state has its own constitution, which divides power between the state's executive, legislative, and judicial branches.

This is a map of California and its counties.

Local Government: Counties

Each state is divided into sections that are usually called **counties**. The functions of counties are different in each state, but they often include law enforcement, judicial administration, road construction and maintenance, public assistance for those in need, and the recording of legal documents.

Local Government: Cities and Towns

▲ This map shows some of the cities and towns in Ventura County, California

Counties can be home to many smaller local governments, including city and town governments. These governments provide many services to their residents, such as maintaining police forces, court systems, hospitals, road and street maintenance, school systems, fire departments, water supply, and garbage disposal. Many of these governments also support museums, libraries, art galleries, and cultural activities.

Political Parties

Among the most influential aspects of today's elections are **political parties**. Political parties are groups of people who share similar opinions about how the government should work. People often vote for **candidates** who are members of a certain political party because they agree with their views and opinions. The voters hope that if their candidates are elected, the government will address the issues they care about most.

The two largest political parties in the United States are the Democratic Party and the Republican Party. About 60 percent of U.S. citizens consider themselves a member of one party or the other. Even those who say they are independent (not a member of either party) often lean strongly toward a particular party.

Democrats and Republicans dominate at almost every level of government. After the 2002 elections, only 3 out of 535 members of

Party Symbols

The Democratic and Republican parties each have an animal as their symbol. The elephant is the symbol of the Republican Party, and the donkey is the symbol of the Democratic Party. Each was originally used to mock the opposing party, but both Democrats and Republicans turned the symbols to their advantage. When Democrat Andrew Jackson ran for president in 1828, people compared him to a donkey because of his stubbornness. Jackson, however, turned the joke around and used the donkey on his campaign posters. The donkey became the unofficial symbol for the Democrats in 1870 when a cartoonist named Thomas Nast used it to represent some Democrats with whom he disagreed. Later, Nast made fun of Republicans in a cartoon that depicted the "Republican vote" as a frightened elephant running away from a donkey wearing a lion's skin. Like Democrats, Republicans also changed the insult into a symbol of their party.

Congress did not belong to one of these two parties. Since 1853, every U.S. president has been either a Republican or a Democrat.

One reason for the strength of the two-party system in the United States is the winner-take-all election system. In other words, the candidate who wins the majority of votes represents the whole area. Even if 49 percent of an area's voters choose a candidate from a different party, those voters do not get to send someone from their party to represent them in government.

The winner-take-all system makes it difficult for **third-party** candidates to enter and win elections. Since voters know that candidates from the two major parties have a much greater chance of winning, they might vote for candidates from these parties even if there is a third-party candidate they like better.

Despite the obstacles faced by third-party candidates, they are an important part of the political landscape. The Democratic and Republican parties are not the original parties, but were formed as "opposition parties." It is possible that a new party could form in the future to meet the growing and changing needs of the population.

▼ Sometimes the participation of a third party can benefit one party by drawing away voters from another. In the 2000 presidential election, some people argued that candidate Ralph Nader (below) caused Vice President Al Gore to lose the election. Third-party candidates like Nader may receive a significant amount of votes, but not nearly enough to win an election.

Primary Elections and Caucuses

In the previous section, you read about the significance of political parties in the U.S. election system. In this section, you will learn how candidates run for office, and what role political parties play in this process.

When someone decides to run for an elected position in government, that person must meet specific requirements. Many government positions require candidates to be at least a certain age and to have lived for a certain amount of time in the area they hope to represent. For some positions, candidates must collect a number of signatures from citizens who support their right to run for office.

▼ The Iowa caucus is particularly important in the presidential race because it takes place before any other caucus or primary election. Politicians and the press look to the Iowa caucus results to get a sense of which two candidates will compete in the national election.

The election process starts with **primary elections**. These are state-level elections in which voters choose a candidate from their political party to run in the final election, called the **general election**. States have different rules about who can vote in primary elections, but the end result is that just one candidate from each party wins.

In some states, voters choose candidates in **caucuses**. Caucuses start with a series of informal meetings between candidates and potential voters. Local party officials then vote on behalf of the voters to select a winner.

In most primary elections, citizens vote directly for candidates. But in presidential primaries, citizens often vote for delegates. Delegates are representatives who promise to vote for a certain presidential candidate at the party's national convention.

Before the presidential election, each of the major political parties holds a national convention. At the national convention, the delegates officially **nominate** their party's candidate for president. They also adopt a party **platform**. A platform is a declaration of the principles and policies supported by the party.

Today, the presidential nominee and the party platform are usually known long before the convention. Even so, national conventions are still viewed as an important event for rallying party members.

▲ Illinois Senator Barack Obama delivers the keynote speech at the 2004 Democratic National Convention in Boston, Massachusetts. Party leaders choose a keynote speaker to deliver the convention's main message and to rally supporters behind the party's presidential candidate.

17

Running a Presidential Campaign

After the political parties have made their nominations official at national conventions, the winning candidates begin to compete with one another in the period leading up to the general election.

Candidates try to persuade people to vote for them by launching a **campaign**. During campaigns, candidates travel around the country and communicate their plan for the government through speeches and interviews. They also participate in **debates** with other candidates. Candidates must work with their staff to make sure that their campaign is represented favorably by the press. Sometimes, candidates make personal attacks against their opponents in order to make them seem incapable of doing a good job. This is called **negative campaigning**.

Incumbents (candidates who are running for re-election) often have an advantage over their opponents. They are already known to many voters, and find it easier to raise money for their campaigns. They have had the chance to perform in office and can often point to accomplishments. However, their time in office can also be used against them by challengers who point out their failures or promise a better future to voters.

A candidate's financial resources can make a big difference in the

▼ Below, George W. Bush and John Kerry participate in a debate during the 2004 election.

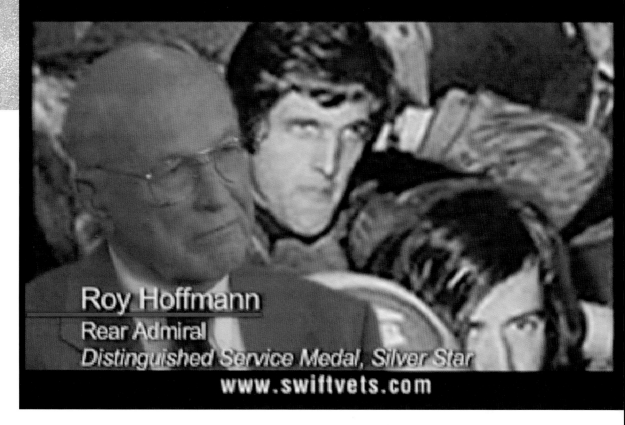

Roy Hoffmann
Rear Admiral
Distinguished Service Medal, Silver Star
www.swiftvets.com

outcome of a campaign. The cost of running a campaign varies depending on the level of government and office. Candidates for local offices spend relatively little, while presidential candidates might spend hundreds of millions of dollars to win an election.

Campaign expenses usually include staff salaries and materials, as well as communication and transportation costs. For many candidates, however, more and more money goes toward television advertisements. From 1972 to 2000, the amount of money spent on television ads increased by 600 percent!

The influence of money on national elections became so significant that in the 1970s, Congress passed laws governing how much money individuals and organizations could give to candidates. Congress placed further limits on contributions in 2002. However, there are no limits on how much candidates themselves can spend on their campaigns. The courts decided that such limits would interfere with a candidate's ability to communicate with the public.

▲ Congress has passed laws aimed at limiting the effect of money on elections. Even so, some groups have found ways to continue raising and spending large sums of money on behalf of candidates they favor. During the 2004 elections, groups such as America Coming Together worked on behalf of Democrats, while the Swift Boat Veterans for Truth worked on behalf of Republicans. Above is a picture from a Swift Boat ad critical of Democratic candidate John Kerry.

National Elections

I n national elections, voters elect the president and vice president, who are part of the executive branch of the government. They also elect members of the two houses of Congress: the **Senate** and the **House of Representatives**. This is called the legislative branch of government. The legislative branch creates and passes new laws.

The Constitution describes the two houses of Congress, the eligibility requirements for their members, and the length of time representatives can serve. It declares that each state should have two senators. Today, there are 50 states, so the Senate has 100 members. All eligible voters in a state can vote for both senators.

According to the Constitution, the number of representatives a state has in the House of Representatives depends on the number of people who live in a state. States with larger populations have more representatives. The House has 435 members.

THE GERRY-MANDER.

Gerrymandering

States with more than one House member divide their state into congressional districts with equal populations. At times, politicians have tried to create districts in a way that would give themselves an advantage in elections. This is called "gerrymandering." Gerrymandering has sometimes resulted in districts of unusual shapes. A clever cartoonist drew this creature based on the shape of a Massachusetts district that was created for political advantage.

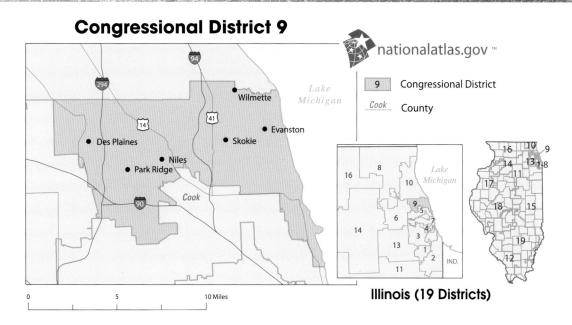

Congressional District 9

nationalatlas.gov ™

9 Congressional District

Cook County

Illinois (19 Districts)

▲ Above are a series of maps showing the location of the 9th Congressional District in Illinois. Notice that there are a higher number of districts in the northeast corner of the state. This is because there is a large population around the city of Chicago.

Elections for members of the House of Representatives are different from those for the Senate. For each representative that a state has in the House, the state creates one **congressional district**. Congressional districts allow citizens to elect a representative familiar with their local needs to represent them in Congress. The number of congressional districts a state has depends on its number of representatives. The citizens of each district vote only to elect their representative.

The Constitution specifies the **term** lengths for all members of government. Presidents serve four-year terms, members of the House serve two-year terms, and senators serve six-year terms.

National elections, in which citizens vote for the president, take place every four years. The election is held on the first Tuesday after the first Monday in November. At the same time as the presidential election, each of the 50 states hold elections for Congress. In between presidential elections, the states hold elections for House members and senators who are up for re-election. These are called mid-term elections because they are held in the middle of the president's term.

21

The Electoral College System

You may be surprised to learn that United States citizens do not directly elect their president. The founders feared that the people might be too uninformed to choose their leaders. One solution was to have Congress choose the president and vice president, but there were problems with this idea, too. In the end, they decided to create the **electoral college**. In this system, citizens vote for **electors**, who then elect the president. This is how presidential elections are still decided today.

According to the Constitution, the number of electors in each state must be equal to the number of its members in Congress. Today there are 538 electors—one for each of the 435 members of the House and 100 senators, and three electors from Washington, D.C. The Constitution allows the state legislatures to decide how to choose their electors.

Electoral College Map

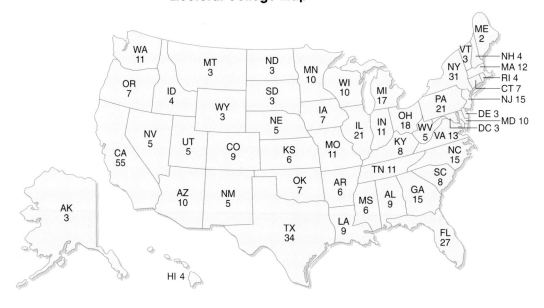

▲ This map shows the number of electoral votes by state.

The votes the electors cast are called electoral votes. To win, a candidate must win at least 270 electoral votes. If no candidate wins a majority of votes, the House of Representatives decides the winner.

In the beginning of December, electors officially cast their votes for president and vice president of the United States. The winners are announced before Congress on January 6, and are sworn into office on January 20. Even though this process happens after the November general election, the votes of individual citizens are still very important. Electors usually vote for the candidate who got the most votes from their states in the general election. This doesn't always happen, however.

It is possible for a presidential candidate to win a majority of the popular votes, yet still lose the election. Such an event occurred in the 1876, 1888, and 2000 presidential elections. In the 2000 election, Vice President Al Gore won by more than 500,000 popular votes, but still lost the election. You will read about this very close election in the next section.

Colorado's Amendment 36

In 2004, the state of Colorado asked its voters to decide on Amendment 36. This amendment would have ended the winner-take-all system for the state's electoral votes. The amendment proposed to divide the state's nine electoral votes according to the percentage of the state's popular vote earned by each presidential candidate. Colorado voters rejected the amendment.

The 2000 Presidential Election

▼ An election official from Broward County, Florida, examines a ballot from the 2000 Presidential election.

The major party candidates in the 2000 presidential election were Republican George W. Bush and Democrat Al Gore. Late on the evening of November 7, 2000, all but Florida's electoral votes had been decided. The winner of Florida's 25 electoral votes would win the presidency. However, the Florida popular vote was too close to call on the night of the election.

Florida election officials finished their count by the next morning. Bush had won by less than 2,000 votes. However, because the vote was so close, Florida election law required that the **ballots** be counted again by machine. Bush's lead narrowed to less than 400 votes.

Gore was concerned with these results. The counting machines had failed to count more than 60,000 ballots. Many voters had not marked their ballots clearly enough for the machines to read. Because so many ballots had not been counted, Gore thought that a hand recount would lead to a more accurate result. He asked election officials to recount the ballots by hand.

Bush believed that a hand recount would be unfair and would break the law. Over the next four weeks, lawyers for both candidates appeared in state and federal courts, trying to gain control over the recount process. Eventually, the case went to the Supreme Court. On December 12, the court decided that Florida would not conduct a hand recount.

▲ Pictured above, George W. Bush is sworn in as the 43rd president of the United States.

The court based its decision on the Fourteenth Amendment, which says that states must treat their citizens equally under the law. The court decided that because Florida counties might have different ways of counting votes, a vote rejected in one county might have been counted in another, and vice versa. Therefore, if Florida were to allow the hand recount to proceed, the state would be treating citizens of different counties unequally.

Finally, on December 18, the electors chosen by each state met to cast their votes for president. On January 2, Congress counted the electoral votes. Bush received 271 and Gore received 267. On January 20, 2001, George W. Bush was sworn in as the 43rd president of the United States.

State and Local Elections

In addition to national elections, each state holds elections for its federal and local governments. Many state and local elections are held on the same day as national elections, in early November.

As you have read, each of the 50 state governments has three branches, just like the federal government. Citizens elect representatives to a state legislature. They also elect a head of the executive branch called a governor. In some states, citizens even vote for judges.

Most states are divided into counties. There are more than 3,000 counties in the United States, many with their own elected officials. At the county level, citizens often elect representatives called county commissioners or supervisors. These and other elected officers perform local tasks such as organizing elections and building and maintaining roads.

This map shows the borders of U.S. counties. The United States has more than 3,000 counties. ▼

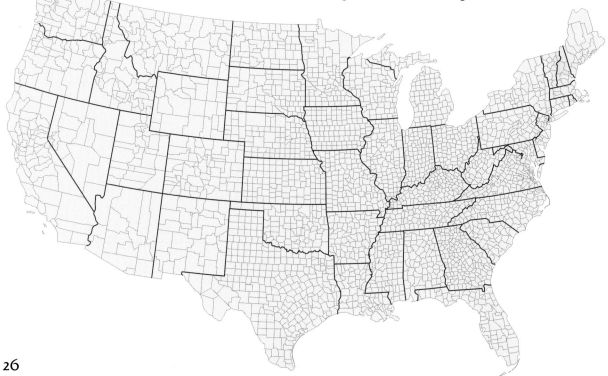

◀ Gray Davis (left) campaigns to hold his position as governor of California in the 2003 recall election.

Counties are often home to a number of other local governments. Among the most important are city governments. The United States was once a nation of farmers. Today, however, about 80 percent of Americans live in towns, large cities, or suburbs.

In cities and towns, people often vote for an executive official called a **mayor**. They also frequently elect representatives to a **city council**, which is a group of people that passes laws for the city. City dwellers depend on local representatives for many of their needs. City governments provide basic services such as police and fire protection, sanitation and trash collection, public transportation, and education.

State and local governments also use forms of direct democracy, which allow the public to participate directly in government. The most common forms are the initiative, the referendum, and the recall.

An initiative is a petition, or request, signed by a certain number of voters. If citizens collect enough signatures to meet state or local requirements, they can require a public vote on a particular proposal or law. A referendum is a direct vote in which the government asks all eligible voters to either accept or reject a proposal or a law.

A recall is the removal of an elected official by voters. This form of direct democracy is allowed by a number of states. In October of 2003, California voters recalled Governor Gray Davis and replaced him with actor Arnold Schwarzenegger.

Election Day

Voting in the United States is a two-step process. In almost every state, citizens first have to register in order to vote. The federal government does not maintain a list of voters. Usually, city or county officials register voters and keep voter lists. City or county officials are also responsible for organizing the second part of the process—the actual election.

Election officials, who are sometimes volunteers, have an enormous job. In addition to registering and keeping lists of voters, officials have to set dates for elections. They must **certify** election candidates and make sure that they meet the minimum requirements. They find locations where people can go to vote, called **polling places**. They also select voting machines, design ballots, and organize large groups of people to oversee the actual voting on Election Day. Finally, election officials oversee the counting of the votes and the certification of the results.

▼ Although many citizens have fought hard for and treasure their voting rights, it is uncommon for all eligible voters to participate in an election.

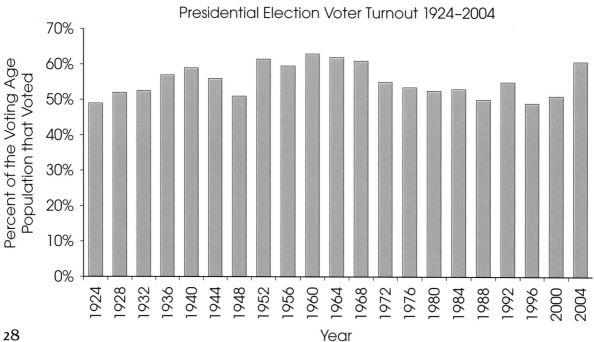

Presidential Election Voter Turnout 1924–2004

Percent of the Voting Age Population that Voted

Year

When a voter arrives at a polling place, he or she presents identification to an election official. The official checks the name on the identification against the voting lists. Eligible voters are given a ballot. A ballot is a sheet of paper that a citizen uses to record his or her vote. Many ballots have a list of the candidates with circles next to their names. Voters mark or pierce the circle next to candidates of their choice. After the election, officials process the ballots with a counting machine that tallies the vote.

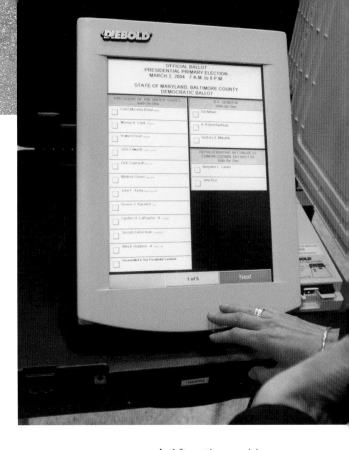

▲ After the problems encountered by voters and election officials in the 2000 election, many counties began to adopt Direct Recording Electronic voting machines (DREs). DREs allow citizens to vote for candidates using computerized touch screens.

Election officials ensure that voting systems are fair and dependable. By establishing people's confidence in the reliability of the voting process, election officials encourage citizens to participate in their government.

Since the 2000 election, state governments have been working to improve voting systems. To avoid some of the problems associated with paper ballots, many counties have begun to use Direct Recording Electronic voting machines (DREs) in their elections. DREs use computerized touch screens to record voters' choices.

The election process hasn't changed much since America's founders decided how it should be done. What has changed is who is allowed to vote and how voting areas are organized. These changes have come about in an effort to make sure that as many people as possible participate in the shaping of our nation. It is the responsibility of every eligible citizen to take part in this vital process of democracy.

Glossary

amendment change or addition to the Constitution

ballot sheet of paper or card used to cast, or make, a vote

campaign organized effort to win election to public office

candidate someone who has qualified and is running for office

caucuses series of meetings in which political parties choose their candidates for public office

certify officially confirm

city council legislative branch of a city

civil rights individual rights of citizens to equal protection under the law and freedom from discrimination; civil rights are guaranteed by the Thirteenth and Fourteenth Amendments to the Constitution

civil rights movement period of history that began in the 1950s in which blacks sought racial equality through nonviolent protest

Congress legislative branch of the United States, which has two houses: the Senate and the House of Representatives

congressional district area into which states are divided for election purposes

constitution document containing a country's basic principles and laws; it describes the powers and duties of the government

county largest administrative division of most U.S. states

debate contest in which two sides argue for opposite sides of an issue

delegate representative

direct democracy democracy in which the public participates in government directly

discrimination unfair treatment of a group of people

elector citizen appointed by a state to vote for the president and vice president

electoral college system in which each state chooses citizens to vote for the president and vice president

executive branch part of the government that carries out and enforces laws

federal system system in which power is divided between a national and state governments

founders individuals who established the government of the United States, especially the authors of the Constitution

general election election in which citizens who are eighteen years old and over can vote for the candidates they want to run the country

governor head of the executive branch of government in a state

House of Representatives lower house of the United States' legislative branch

incumbent official who currently holds office and is running for re-election

judicial branch part of the government that interprets the law

legislative branch part of the government that makes laws

mayor head of the executive branch of government in a city or town

national convention gathering at which a national political party adopts a platform and nominates its candidates for president and vice president

negative campaigning trying to win an election by saying negative things about an opponent's personality or record

nominate suggest a person for appointment or election to a position

platform official statement of the principles and policies supported by a political party

political party group of people who have similar views about government

polling place location, such as a school or church, where people go to vote

primary election election in which political parties choose their candidates for public offices

register officially sign up to vote

representative democracy government in which citizens exercise power by choosing people to represent them in the government

Senate upper house of the United States' legislative branch

suffrage right to vote

term length of time, set by law, served by an elected person

third party political party that operates in opposition to the two main political parties in a two-party system

Union term used to describe the United States

Voting Rights Act law passed by Congress in 1965 to ensure the voting rights of blacks

Further Reading

Giesecke, Ernestine. *National Government*. Chicago: Heinemann Library, 2000.

Giesecke, Ernestine. *State Government*. Chicago: Heinemann Library, 2000.

Giesecke, Ernestine. *Local Government*. Chicago: Heinemann Library, 2000.

Granfield, Linda. *America Votes: How Our President is Elected.* Tonawanda, New York: Kids Can Press, 2003.

Gutman, Dan. *Landslide!: A Kid's Guide to the U.S. Elections.* New York: Simon & Schuster, 2000.

Landau, Elaine. *The 2000 Presidential Election*. Chicago: Children's Press, 2002.

Index